▪ POCKET SERIES ▪

Charlie Chaplin

By Dylan George

Contents

■ POCKET SERIES ■

First published in the UK in 2010
By Instinctive Product Development

© Instinctive Product Development 2010

Publishers: Vanessa Gardner and Carl Edwards

Printed and bound in China

ISBN: 978-1-907657-23-8

Designed by: BrainWave

Creative Director: Kevin Gardner

Written by Dylan George

Images courtesy of MirrorPix, Shutterstock and
Wiki Commons

Introduction

**"A day without laughter
is a day wasted."**

That was the philosophy of Charlie
Chaplin, one of the greatest entertainers
the world has ever seen, and the medical
profession have often agreed, declaring
that humour has fantastic healing
properties encouraging people to laugh –
or at least smile – every day. It is perhaps
difficult for today's younger generation to
comprehend that the earliest of Chaplin's
silent movies are approaching 100 years
old. Yet, even these soon to be centurions
still possess an energetic vigour that
moviemakers strive to match in the
21st Century.

   Chaplin's origins date back to London
at the tail end of the 19th Century and
a childhood that was fragmented with
hardship and sorrow. He was denied the

foundation of a stable family environment and was forced to eke out a living from a very early age by whatever means he could… whether that was in his preferred environment of the theatre or in more conservative and traditional surroundings. His elder brother Sydney was at his side during his formative years and the two were extremely close throughout their lives. Despite this inauspicious start, Charlie triumphed over adversity and landed in America determined to make his own fame and fortune.

This he achieved in a few short years having accidentally stumbled upon a character that would take the world by storm while preparing for his second cinematic engagement. Randomly picking an outfit that included big shoes, a hat that was too small, baggy trousers and a walking cane thrown in as an afterthought, "The Tramp" had arrived on stage and silver screen. Chaplin topped off the persona with a unique "toothbrush" moustache and an enduring

legend was born. He was all set to take Hollywood and the rest of the world by storm and he didn't disappoint.

It wasn't long before Chaplin added writing and directing to his already impressive résumé and he soon became

7

Hollywood's most prominent star. Even when contracts were due to expire, he never failed to find an alternative employer – such was the clamour for his talents. The 1910s and 1920s were a very prolific period in the silent movie industry, so much so that – despite slowing down as age advanced – Charlie Chaplin's career list of films tops the 80 mark.

But it was not all sweetness and light for Chaplin. It took him three dress rehearsals before he found the love of his life in the form of Oona, and they went on to marry and have eight children between 1944 and 1962. The pair were inseparable for the remainder of Charlie's life and Oona was a constant support through the difficult years when her husband was accused of being a Communist sympathiser at a time when America was paranoid over the creeping influence of the Soviet Union.

It led to him being exiled for the last 25 years of his life, a situation that the Chaplins initially found hard to stomach.

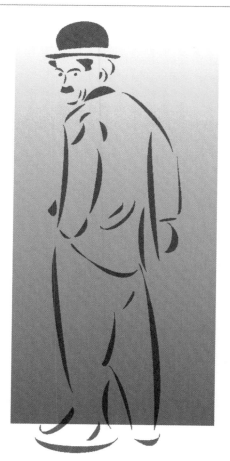

They soldiered on, however, and made a new life in Switzerland where they found the peace and tranquillity that had been impossible to attain in the hustle and bustle of Hollywood. His alleged sins eventually proved unfounded, Charlie Chaplin was honoured at the 1972 Academy Awards and received recognition from the country of his birth in the form of a knighthood three years later. In spite of the irony of knighting a "tramp", it was a fitting tribute to one of Great Britain's finest exports and fans still watch his films with millions of new converts joining the throng more than 30 years after his death.

Even though some of his films were not well received at the time of their release, looking back most will concede that each and every one is worthy of praise – some perhaps more than others – and provide a suitable legacy to the life and career of the one and only Sir Charlie Chaplin…

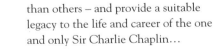

■ **ABOVE RIGHT:** What will Charlie Chaplin look like today?

10

Early Life

"The saddest thing I can imagine is to get used to luxury."

A life of luxury would have been a complete pipedream for the young Charlie Chaplin… even after it had been foretold that he would be the most famous person in the world. Life was tough for the Chaplin family in 19th Century London but few could have predicted that the "prophecy" would be fulfilled in such a way.

Charles Spencer Chaplin was born in East Street, Walworth, on 16 April 1889. His father was an entertainer by trade but an alcoholic by nature. A reasonably successful singer and actor before hitting the bottle, Charles Chaplin Sr's career went into a downward spiral and he played little part in raising the boys having separated from Charlie's mother

■ **LEFT:** The home of Charlie Chaplin in Kennington where he spent the early years of his life.

11

before his son's third birthday.

Charlie's mother, Hannah Hill Chaplin, was also a music hall entertainer being a talented pianist, singer and actress in her own right but she suffered from mental illness. Sydney (born on 16 March 1885) was the product of a previous relationship but was raised by Charles Sr following his marriage to Hannah in June 1885. She went on to give birth to a third son, George Wheeler Dryden, on 31 August 1892 and it was

■ **ABOVE:** Charlie Chaplin on set.

13

her adulterous relationship with his father – another music hall entertainer, named Leo Dryden – that resulted in her marriage to Charles failing beyond repair. Sydney and Charlie continued to live with their mother but George was raised by his father and would remain a secret half-brother for a number of years. Sydney and Charlie discovered their half-brother's existence after Charlie had achieved worldwide fame in the 1910s. Wheeler was also an actor and the brothers reunited in Hollywood in 1918, occasionally working together at Chaplin's studio during the 1950s.

Charlie clearly inherited his love of entertaining from his parents, in particular a love of singing and an imposing presence onstage. He had his first taste of public performance in January 1894 when he accompanied his mother to an Army theatre in Aldershot, Hampshire. She was suffering from a larynx condition and was unable to perform, with the audience booing her offstage and throwing things at her. Little Charlie bravely took her place on the stage and gave a heart-warming rendition of "Jack Jones", a popular tune of the era. A star was born…

The following year, however, Hannah suffered a mental breakdown and the family entered the Lambeth Workhouse in June 1896. It wasn't long before the three were separated, with the boys being sent to Hanwell School for Orphans and Destitute Children.

It was the beginning of a childhood spent in orphanages for the two brothers, although they did go to live with their father and his mistress for a while in 1898 after Hannah had suffered yet another breakdown. It was a particularly difficult time for the boys as they were often beaten and were constantly hungry. Their father's mistress sent them to Archbishop Temples Boys School but Charlie finished his education being barely able to read or write. As it turned out, the next few years would have a dramatic effect on the boys' lives as

Charles Sr died of cirrhosis of the liver in May 1901 while Hannah was to spend the rest of her life in various institutions before her death in August 1928.

Syd had been placed in a programme designed to train young boys to become seaman, on a training ship docked at Grays, Essex. He followed this with several years spent working on ships but his ambition was to get into the entertainment business and he left his final voyage with that in mind. At the time of his father's death, Charlie was living in Lambeth and was one of The Eight Lancashire Lads, a group of male dancers.

He had spent as much of his youth as possible in earning his keep as a performer (miming, acting in circuses and even clog dancing) but is also reported to have had several "proper" jobs including working in a barber's shop, a doctor's office, a printing plant and a stationery store to extricate himself from a life in orphanages and workhouses. It was this diversity seen at a tender age plus the memories of a hard upbringing that would provide Charlie with the inspiration for many of his comical but mainly melancholy plots once he began writing his own films.

The two brothers did get to perform onstage together in a theatre production of *Sherlock Holmes* in the mid 1900s in which Syd was cast as a villain and Charlie played a paperboy. In 1906, however, Syd landed a contract with Fred Karno's troupe of comedians and was instrumental in Charlie's introduction to the company two years later. By then, Syd had risen through the ranks and was one of the principal comedians, overshadowing his younger brother for the only time in their career. By the time Charlie was 19, though, he had forged a reputation as one of the most popular music hall entertainers in the country after his talent for comic mime developed.

Charlie and his fellow performers went

■ **ABOVE:** Stan Laurel.

to the United States in 1910 on a two-year tour of a production entitled *A Night in an English Music Hall* and he quickly fell in love with both the country and the burgeoning motion picture industry.

Chaplin instantly saw the early potential of motion pictures and recognised the appeal they would have to audiences. Indeed, he even discussed setting up a partnership with tour manager Alf

■ **ABOVE:** Keystone Studios, otherwise known as Sennett Studios, circa 1917.

Reeves, whereby they would buy their own camera to film the troupe and then market the resulting film. In the end, there simply wasn't enough time during the show's hectic schedule for them to bring their proposal to fruition although Reeves remained a lifelong friend and later served as manager for Chaplin's film studio. This foray into producing commercially viable films did, however, demonstrate that even at this early stage Charlie had a passion for the cinema that surpassed simply being an actor.

A second US tour in October 1912 saw Charlie sharing a room in a boarding house with a certain Arthur Stanley Jefferson… a fellow Englishman who would go on to fame and fortune in his own right as Stan Laurel, one half of the legendary comedy duo Laurel and Hardy. It was during this tour that Keystone Films' Mack Sennett – on a date with Mabel Normand, who would later appear in several productions with Chaplin – caught the show and Charlie's

headline-grabbing performance stuck in his mind. He later contacted the troupe with an offer of employment but Chaplin remained with the Karno Troupe until December 1913 to see his contract out after which he was instructed to report to the Keystone Studios in Los Angeles. The contract he agreed with Keystone's Adam Kessel was worth $150 per week and doubled his previous salary.

Chaplin's first venture into the art of motion pictures did not run smoothly, however, and there are reports that he had difficulty adjusting and was averse to being directed by a woman (Mabel Normand). His debut came in February 1914 with the release of *Making a Living* but Sennett in particular was concerned he had made a mistake. Luckily, for the millions of fans, Chaplin was given a second chance and demonstrated his comic genius.

Charlie picked his own costume for his second outing on celluloid, *Kid Auto Races at Venice*, deciding upon an

overstated outfit that included baggy trousers, big shoes, a cane and a derby hat. Everything was a contradiction: the trousers too big; the coat too tight; the hat too small; and the shoes too large. As Chaplin explained, it was a moment of inspiration: "I had no idea of the character. But the moment I was dressed, the clothes and the make-up made me feel the person he was. I began to know him, and by the time I walked onto the stage he was fully born."

In just three months, Chaplin's star was rising high and he was proving himself a box office hit. Buoyed by this rise in popularity, Charlie put forward a proposal that he direct his own productions. To protect the studio against potential failure, he offered to put up his $1,500 life savings as security to cover any film that did not make a profit. After 10 films as an actor, *Twenty Minutes of Love* – released in April 1914 – saw Chaplin's debut as a director and the rest, as they say, is history…

■ **RIGHT:** Charlie with Douglas Fairbanks, Mary Pickford and D W Griffith.

10086
SUNSET B

10096
HOLLYWOOD

Hollywood and the Silver Screen

> "I went into the business for the money, and the art grew out of it. If people are disillusioned by that remark, I can't help it. It's the truth."

Having recognised his true value to Keystone, Charlie Chaplin opened negotiations with Sennett as his one-year contract drew to a close. He believed he was worth $1,000 per week, an offer that his boss declined but it is alleged that Chaplin was offered a partnership although nothing ever became of this. As a result, Charlie saw out the remaining four months of his contract in a state of

23

■ **ABOVE:** A Charlie Chaplin lookalike competition.

limbo, unsure where his career was headed.

When Charlie had been negotiating his Keystone contract, he had suggested that his elder brother was also invited to join the company. Syd duly arrived in October 1914 and did make a few comedies before essentially "retiring" to concentrate on handling the majority of his brother's business affairs. The pair did at one point discuss the idea of forming their own company but, with Syd still contracted to Keystone, Charlie signed for the Essanay Film Manufacturing Company in January 1915 on a handsome $1,250 per week plus a $10,000 signing-on bonus with the brief to make 14 films in the coming year.

The first films that Chaplin worked on for his new employer did not prove a pleasant experience and he asked for permission to work in Los Angeles rather than Chicago or San Francisco. This was eventually granted and meant that Charlie and Syd – now free from Keystone – could collaborate to

great effect. Syd proved to have a particularly astute business brain and made recommendations to Essanay that increased each film's returns resulting in a renegotiated contract that rewarded Charlie with a $10,000 bonus for each picture.

Essanay cashed in on Chaplin's status and launched a range of merchandise in 1915 that ensured their brightest star was in the faces and minds of the public in general,

■ **ABOVE RIGHT:** Walt Disney.

not just those who frequented cinemas. There were even nationwide contests where amateurs could compete to provide the best impersonation of Charlie Chaplin and some of the young hopefuls included Walt Disney (1901-1966) and Bob Hope (1903-2003).

But Charlie Chaplin's greatest benefit of his newfound fame and his newly negotiated deal was that it allowed him time to perfect his craft. Instead of churning out short comedies week after week after week, he could concentrate on improving the quality of his offerings and continue his development. Charlie became somewhat of a perfectionist – no longer was he required to accept the first take, he could reshoot the scene until he was satisfied.

This resulted in much better – and more critically acclaimed – productions and *The Tramp*, released in April 1915, is generally regarded as the first of his many masterpieces. Inspired by some of his contemporaries, Chaplin began to bring

more emotion to his creations instead of just concentrating on the comedy aspect although the generic underdog triumphing over adversity remained an underlying current.

Once his contract expired, Chaplin tried to negotiate a new deal that would see him paid $500,000 but Essanay were not initially forthcoming with a signature and so Sydney began to find alternative employment for his brother. February 1916 saw Charlie sign with Mutual Films for a weekly salary of $10,000 and a

■ **ABOVE:** Bob Hope.
■ **RIGHT:** Charlie Chaplin sat at his desk.

$150,000 signing-on bonus (half of which he gave to Sydney in recognition of his role in the process).

Mutual rented a Hollywood studio for the 26-year-old Chaplin to work in and much of his output during this period is rightly regarded as some of his best. Films such as *The Floorwalker*, *The Cure*, *Easy Street*, *The Pawnshop* and *The Adventurer* can all lay claim to be Chaplin masterpieces and Mutual themselves were so pleased with his creations during his initial contract that they offered him $1 million for his next 12 films. Chaplin, however, was still not satisfied with the number of films that he was required to produce in a year and decided to form his own production company and signed a contract with First National in June 1917 to produce eight two-reel films. Chaplin's recompense for this would be a total of $1.25 million and he began an ambitious expansion of his art that encompassed longer films such as *Shoulder Arms*, *The Pilgrim* and *The Kid*.

Despite the success that Chaplin brought to First National, they were reluctant to negotiate a new contract and the reason eventually became apparent when it was announced they were merging with Paramount. Many stars feared the consequences of this union that threatened to cap their salaries and squeeze independent production companies like Chaplin's out of existence.

Many of his fellow A-list stars found themselves in a similar predicament and so – with Mary Pickford, Douglas Fairbanks, William S Hart and D W Griffith – Chaplin co-founded United Artists. Chaplin would serve on the board until the 1950s, long after many of his partners had retired. The name of the quintet's distribution company was a clear indication of their mutual commitment to escape the claustrophobic grip of the established Hollywood powerhouses but Charlie first had to honour his obligation to First National and this, coupled with the strain of a decaying first

■ **ABOVE:** Signing of the contract establishing United Artists in 1919.

■ **ABOVE:** Charlie Chaplin during 1921 European Tour.

became the favoured location for the silent film stars of the era, and lived there from its completion in 1923 until his fateful trip to London in 1952.

Under the United Artists umbrella, Chaplin found more freedom to indulge his creative genius without having to adhere to the hectic production line that had been forced upon him during his earlier career. As a result, his first UA production, A Woman of Paris (1923), was not exactly what his public expected in that it was a psychological drama. It was not a box office smash but the follow-up was.

The Gold Rush was released in June 1925 and went on to become Chaplin's most successful silent movie, eventually taking a colossal $4 million. Lita Grey, Chaplin's second wife, had been cast as the leading lady but when she became pregnant, she was replaced by Georgia Hale. The film was described by Charlie as the one he'd most like to be remembered for and contained classic

marriage, hampered the start-up venture's honeymoon period and also had an adverse effect on his creativity.

It was around this time that – despite having been content since his arrival in the States to rent his living accommodation – Charlie was finally persuaded by his friends to put down permanent roots on his return from a 1921 European Tour. Chaplin designed the house he wanted built in Summit Drive, once an open hillside that soon

■ **ABOVE:** Douglas Fairbanks and Mary Pickford.

■ **ABOVE:** The London premiere of *City Lights*.

the change in public attitude following his public divorce from Grey – resulted in production of his next film being halted while he recovered from a nervous breakdown. Such was the strain on him that his hair dramatically turned white in a very short period of time. Filming resumed in September for *The Circus* and it was well received by both critics and movie audiences when it was released the following January. It performed well at the box office – generating $3 million – and restored some of his credibility within the industry.

But the industry was advancing in parallel to technological advances and 1927 had also seen the release of *The Jazz Singer*. While numerous short films had utilised recorded sound in the form of music and effects, this was the first feature film advertised as a talking picture or "talkie" and contained dialogue. Chaplin initially resisted the temptation to incorporate the new technology into his films.

moments such as the Little Tramp having to eat his boot (actually a prop made of liquorice) and making two bread rolls stabbed with forks into a table-top dance.

The year of 1927 was not a particularly happy time for Charlie Chaplin both personally and professionally. He stood accused by the federal authorities of tax evasion to the sum of $1.3 million and the stresses he had to endure – as well as

■ **ABOVE:** Lita Grey.

"Talkies are spoiling the oldest art in the world," he exclaimed, "the art of pantomime. They are ruining the great beauty of silence. They are defeating the meaning of the screen."

Although he was excited about the opportunity of matching the onscreen action to a musical score, *City Lights* (1931) and *Modern Times* (1936) were in effect mute and became his final two silent movies.

The former again impressed the critics, with one journalist later claiming that it was "the greatest single piece of acting ever committed to celluloid". It boasted a delicate recipe of comedy and sentimentality and took more than 530 days to complete but Chaplin was aware that he "had worked himself into a neurotic state of wanting perfection" in his desire to compete with his creation's talking counterparts of the 1930s. Its success inspired him to produce his last silent masterpiece: *Modern Times*. Set in the Industrial Age, it represented

the Little Tramp's final outing and is a comment on the desperate employment and fiscal conditions many people faced during the Great Depression; conditions created, in Chaplin's view, by the efficiencies of modern industrialisation. While it is definitely considered a

■ **ABOVE:** *The Great Dictator.*

silent movie, *Modern Times* does have a certain sound element – to appease audiences becoming more acclimatised to talkies – and represents the first time that Chaplin's voice was heard on film. This was achieved by using equipment such as a TV monitor or a radio, while Chaplin himself is heard singing a nonsense song at the end.

Unfortunately, it proved to be his first feature film that was not classed as a blockbuster so he jumped on the audio bandwagon for the follow up. Many argue that *The Great Dictator* – Chaplin's personal vehicle of defiance against the Nazi regime – is a masterpiece but it aired to mixed reviews in a country that did not want to involve itself in the fight

■ **ABOVE:** Mahatma Gandhi with Charlie Chaplin in 1931.

Chaplin's final pair of Hollywood productions were unable to hit the heights that their predecessors had achieved. *Monsieur Verdoux* – based on a suggestion by Orson Welles – was a black comedy released in April 1947 that seemed to focus on capitalism in a critical light while *Limelight* (1952) was far less political and became a family affair. Chaplin prominently featured members of his family in the film, including five of his children and his half-brother Wheeler Dryden, while the pairing of Chaplin with Buster Keaton in the final musical number is historic for being the only time the two appeared on film together.

Such was his state of mind that, despite being pleased with the finished article, Chaplin allegedly told his older sons that he expected *Limelight* to be his last film. As a result, he happily returned to the country of his birth for the UK premiere of *Limelight* in 1952 but little did he realise that it would be 20 years before he again stepped on American soil…

against German oppression. It had been pointed out to Chaplin that the Little Tramp bore some resemblance to Adolf Hitler and a suggested case of mixed identity was mooted. Filming actually commenced before the outbreak of the Second World War but it was eventually released in October 1940, more than a year after the conflict had begun in Europe. Nevertheless, the film was nominated for three Academy Awards but failed to win any golden statues.

■ **ABOVE LEFT:** Buster Keaton with son and grandsons.

■ **ABOVE:** Charlie with J Arthur Rank.

Family and Children

> "Nothing is permanent in
> this wicked world – not even
> our troubles."

Charlie Chaplin's personal life seemed
at times to mirror those of his alter egos
on the silver screen in that the course of
true love never ran smoothly. An early
infatuation with Hetty Kelly, a dancer in
London, was unrequited; Chaplin (then
19) felt it was love at first sight while
the 15-year-old Hetty was not ready for
a long-term relationship. It did, however,
give Charlie a picture of his ideal girl and
it is alleged that he had a tendency to use
lookalike actresses in his films.

One of his leading ladies was Edna
Purviance, who caught his eye in 1915,
although he apparently believed her too

■ **LEFT:** Edna Purviance.

serious and morose for comedy. Edna was 19 when she signed for Chaplin but while she was ready for commitment, Chaplin was already "married" to his work and the relationship had ceased to exist by early 1918 although the pair would forever be close friends. Little did Chaplin know, however, that by the end of that year he would be married.

Charlie met the girl who would become the first Mrs Chaplin at a party in early 1918 and they dated for several months before rumours began that they had married. There is nothing unusual these days for celebrities to tie the knot in private but the gossip mill was working overtime because Mildred Harris was just 16 years old. It is alleged that Mildred (born 29 November 1901) told Charlie that she was pregnant and they married on 23 October 1918. As it turned out, she wasn't expecting at that time although it wasn't long before she was. The couple proudly announced the birth of Norman Spencer Chaplin on 7 July 1919 but sadly

their son died three days later and it was only a matter of time before the marriage suffered the same fate. With Chaplin focussing on his work and Mildred unwilling to accept his dedication to his trade, the couple divorced on 13 November 1920. Mildred went on to date the then Prince of Wales and was twice married before dying of pneumonia in July 1944.

Lillita McMurray (born 15 April 1908) became Charlie's second wife on 26 November 1924 in a ceremony that again sparked moral outrage because of her tender years. He had known her for four years, having been introduced by his assistant director who lived next door to her family, but it wasn't until after he signed her – under a new stage name of Lita Grey – as his new leading lady in March 1924 that romance began to blossom. As had happened the first time around, it wasn't long before his wife gave birth (Charles Chaplin Jr on 5 May 1925) although, this time, their

■ **ABOVE:** Mildred Harris, Charlie's first wife.

son survived. A second son, Sydney, arrived the following March, but by the end of 1926 the marriage had stumbled upon stony ground due to a number of alleged affairs on Charlie's part and a bitter public divorce ensued. This was finalised on 22 August 1927 and resulted in Charlie being ordered to pay $600,000 with $100,000 in trust for each of his sons, the largest divorce settlement of that era. Lita would marry three more times before passing away from cancer in December 1995.

Such was the distress caused by the end of his second marriage that Charlie's relationship with Lita barely rated a mention in his 1964 biography and it would be almost 10 years before he settled again. This time, however, there was no hint of a scandal over a teenage bride although Pauline Levy (born 3 June 1910) – more famous under her stage name of Paulette Goddard – was more than 20 years his junior. She was already a divorcée by the time they met after

Chaplin's World Tour of 1931-32 but they clicked and friendship soon transformed into love. Chaplin realised that Paulette would only enhance his forthcoming feature, *Modern Times*, and cast her as Ellen Peterson, a *gamine* (French meaning urchin, waif or playful, naughty child). The 1936 film was a success and made a star of Paulette in the same year that Chaplin claimed the pair married on a trip to China. Chaplin's third marriage is something of a mystery as he reportedly informed close friends that they were just a common-law husband and wife who had never officially tied the knot.

■ **ABOVE:** Pauline Levy, better known as Paulette Goddard.

■ **ABOVE:** With Sophia Loren and son, Sydney.

Whatever the truth, this relationship proved to be Chaplin's most enduring so far but even this failed to last the distance. Cracks began to show during the filming of *The Great Dictator* and the pair were "divorced" in Mexico on 4 June 1942. Paulette and Charlie remained friends and both ended up living in Switzerland although they did not meet. Paulette married twice more and died of emphysema in Switzerland in April 1990.

As had previously occurred, Charlie met the future Mrs Chaplin while seeking to replace Paulette as his leading lady. This time, though, it would be a true and everlasting love that came from the audition. Oona O'Neill (born 14 May 1925) had travelled from New York to try to make it as an actress in Hollywood and met Chaplin in late 1942. The movie legend signed her to his books and she began taking acting lessons but plans for the proposed *Shadow and Substance* film fell by the wayside and the couple married in Santa Barbara on 16 June 1943.

■ **ABOVE:** Charlie Chaplin with wife Oona, Michael, Geraldine, Josephine and Victoria.

The following decade saw the Chaplins produce another four children – Victoria, Eugene, Jane and Annette – while Christopher made his debut in 1962 when his father was the grand old age of 73. Their marriage survived the darkest moments of Charlie's life and career including enforced exile from his adopted home of the United States.

While being the doting father, it has been reported that Charlie found it difficult to talk to his offspring about his early career and fame but that did not prevent their home in Switzerland being frequented by many a famous visitor. It was Oona, though, who made the trip to the US to tie up the loose ends of their life in the States. She closed and packed up her husband's studio as well as the family home – including the priceless legacy of a lifetime in motion pictures. Indeed, it is as a result of Oona's foresight that Charlie Chaplin's films can be enjoyed in the 21st Century and a special film vault was constructed at their Swiss home.

The majority of friends, as well as public and critics alike, thought the marriage was doomed to repeat the failure of his previous relationships – especially with the 36-year age gap – but they were all proved wrong. Charlie's first daughter, Geraldine, arrived the following year and was soon followed by Michael and Josephine before the end of the 1940s.

46

■ **ABOVE LEFT:** Geraldine, daughter of Charlie Chaplin.
■ **RIGHT:** Geraldine Chaplin at Cannes.

Such was Oona's dedication to her husband that she relinquished her American citizenship and concentrated on life in exile. But she was always there for Charlie on the few trips he did take in later life and was a constant companion during his final years in Switzerland. After Charlie's death in December 1977, Oona's life lost its main purpose and she even relocated to New York; perhaps the happy memories of her 34-year marriage were too much to bear in the Swiss family home.

Despite the heartbreak, Oona lived until 27 September 1991 before succumbing to cancer and being buried next to her beloved husband but not before she gave her approval for filming of the biopic *Chaplin*. Many of Charlie Chaplin's descendants have tried their hand at acting over the years, none more so than his eldest daughter Geraldine who got to play the part of Hannah Chaplin, Charlie's mother and her grandmother…

■ **ABOVE:** Michael Chaplin.

Charlie Chaplin (1889-1977) Family Tree

Parents
Charles Spencer Chaplin Sr (1863-1901)
Hannah Chaplin (1866-1928)

Siblings
Sydney Chaplin (1885-1965)
George Wheeler Dryden (1892-1957)

Wives
Mildred Harris (1901-1944)
Lita Grey (1908-1995)
Paulette Goddard (1910-1990)
Oona O'Neill (1925-1991)

Children
Norman Spencer Chaplin (1919-1919)
Charles Chaplin Jr (1925-1968)
Sydney Earle Chaplin (1926-2009)
Geraldine Chaplin (1944-)
Michael Chaplin (1946-)
Josephine Chaplin (1949-)
Victoria Chaplin (1951-)
Eugene Anthony Chaplin (1953-)
Jane Cecil Chaplin (1957-)
Annette Emily Chaplin (1959-)
Christopher Chaplin (1962-)

Grandchildren
Susan Maree Chaplin
Stephan Chaplin
Shane Saura Chaplin
Oona Chaplin
Kathleen Chaplin
Dolores Chaplin
Carmen Chaplin
George Chaplin
Julien Ronet
Aurélia Thiérrée
James Thiérrée
Kiera Chaplin
Orson Salkind
Osceola Salkind

Great Grandchildren
Laurissa Maree Chaplin Newton
Allison Mary Chaplin Newton
Tyler David Chaplin Newton
Casey Jackson Chaplin Newton
Tamara Chaplin

49

50

Later Life and Legacy

"I don't believe that the public knows what it wants; this is the conclusion that I have drawn from my career."

While Chaplin had been a keen supporter of the Allied effort during the First World War, his refusal to adopt a similar stance during the second global conflict led to public anger. Added to this were the political overtures of his films released during the preceding decade. *Modern Times* portrayed a grim picture of the working population while the final speech in *The Great Dictator* criticised those who blindly followed their nation's leaders and both clearly demonstrated his political views.

But the main controversy that

■ **LEFT:** J Edgar Hoover.

dogged him in the mid 1940s was the aftermath of his relationship with Joan Barry. Chaplin had had a brief fling with the actress in 1942-43 but it was ended once she started showing signs of mental illness that brought back memories of his mother. Barry gave birth to a daughter, Carol Ann, on 2 October 1943 and filed a paternity suit against Chaplin, claiming he was the father. Charlie agreed to take a blood test that proved he wasn't the girl's biological father but Barry's lawyer convinced the court that these tests were inadmissible evidence and the ruling went against him. Chaplin was ordered to support Carol Ann, although the case proved to be the catalyst for a later change in California law. Chaplin was also charged in 1944 with offences towards Barry under the Mann Act that prohibits white slavery and the interstate transport of females for "immoral purposes". He was later acquitted of these allegations but the trial damaged his reputation beyond repair.

■ **LEFT:** Orson Welles.

But it was the American fear of Communism that would have an irreversible effect on the life of Charlie Chaplin. Despite having been a world famous entertainer and a US resident since 1914, although he had never officially become a citizen, Chaplin was accused of "un-American activities" and labelled a suspected Communist. It was the era of McCarthyism – a period in US history also known as the Second Red Scare – that lasted from the late 1940s to the late 1950s. Originally coined to criticise the anti-Communist pursuits of US Senator Joseph McCarthy, it was characterised by heightened fears of Communist influence on American institutions and espionage by Soviet agents.

FBI Director J Edgar Hoover ordered that secret files be compiled dissecting Chaplin and his life in an effort to terminate his US residency. Chaplin's support for a second European Front to assist the Soviet Union in 1942 had been widely criticised as many believed it painted him as a Red but the pressure increased in the late 1940s and several prominent members of Congress considered calling him as a witness in the hearings. Other victims of this American paranoia included luminaries from the world of stage and screen such as Orson Welles, Edward G Robinson and Arthur Miller not to mention Burgess Meredith who had married Chaplin's third wife, Paulette Goddard.

Faced with an embarrassing absence

■ **ABOVE:** Edward G Robinson.

■ **ABOVE:** Arthur Miller with wife, Marilyn Monroe.

of proof or witnesses to support their allegations, the FBI were forced to admit on 29 December 1948 that they had no evidence to support their belief that Chaplin was a Communist but Hoover saw his opportunity in September 1952 with Chaplin's trip to the United Kingdom. He leaned on the Immigration and Naturalisation Service to revoke Chaplin's entry permit on the grounds of his alleged political views. As a result, Charlie was stranded in the UK – an exile from his home of nearly 40 years – and, making the following statement, decided that he could not return to the States.

"Since the end of the last World War," he complained, "I have been the object of lies and propaganda by powerful reactionary groups who, by their influence and by the aid of America's yellow press, have created an unhealthy atmosphere in which liberal-minded individuals can be singled out and persecuted. Under these conditions I

find it virtually impossible to continue my motion picture work, and I have therefore given up my residence in the United States."

It wasn't the end of the road for Chaplin's film career, however, though his final two offerings – made in

London – were not the box office hits of yesteryear. Released in 1957, *A King in New York*, seemed an open attack on the Stateside regime and its way of life that brought a fresh wave of pro-Communism accusations. Chaplin's final film a decade later, *A Countess from Hong Kong*, starred Sophia Loren and Marlon Brando but was labelled a disaster by the critics. It did, however, mark Charlie Chaplin's final screen appearance as he made a cameo as a seasick steward. A golden era was truly over.

Charlie and Oona had decided to settle in Switzerland and bought a lakeside home in Corsier sur Vevey in January 1953. They sold all their possessions in the United States and spent the remainder of the 1950s and 1960s raising their family but mourned the passing of Sydney Chaplin on 16 April 1965, ironically Charlie's 76th birthday. By the 1970s, however, attitudes had changed.

Charlie and Oona were invited to the Academy Awards in 1972 so that the "Little Tramp" could be honoured with a special Oscar for his contribution to the motion picture industry. Many people who had worked with Chaplin during his career turned up to see him in either New

■ **ABOVE:** Front page news.

■ **ABOVE:** Charlie Chaplin in London, 1952.

York or Los Angeles and the strength of adulation from the public did not pass the star by unnoticed. It was an emotional trip for both husband and wife. Charlie made one last visit to his old film studio but was unable to bring himself to go in and just stood at the entry gate gazing at the remnants of a previous life.

The Chaplins returned to London in 1975 when he was made a Knight Commander of the British Empire… arise Sir Charlie! But his advanced years were taking their toll on his physical strength and an embarrassed Chaplin asked photographers not to capture him on film struggling into the waiting car. It's easy to empathise with the Hollywood legend who wanted to preserve his dignity and ensure that his fans remembered him at his best in what would turn out to be his final public goodbye.

Chaplin completed the restoration of his classic films in 1976 with the final one being a particular favourite of his (*A Woman of Paris*) but the star's health

was taking a turn for the worst. He drifted through the final year of his life in a wheelchair, taking walks or drives, receiving visitors and family but was housebound by November 1977. All the while, his devoted Oona cared for Charlie but even she could not prevent him from slipping his mortal coil when he died peacefully in his sleep on Christmas Day 1977.

■ **ABOVE:** Standing with Winston Churchill in 1954.

■ **ABOVE:** Sir Charlie Chaplin with wife Oona.

Fans left flowers at the gates of his former film studios as well as at the grave of his mother in Hollywood's Memorial Cemetery in Los Angeles. Charlie Chaplin was buried in his local Swiss cemetery but thieves stole his corpse on 1 March 1978 with the intention of extorting money from his family. His body was recovered 11 weeks later, however, and the culprits caught but it was decided that, to prevent any further such atrocity, his coffin should be entombed under six feet of concrete to ensure the Little Tramp's eternal peace.

Charlie Chaplin's legacy lives on through his family and his lifetime in motion pictures among other avenues. Computer manufacturer IBM used an impersonator to sell their machines during a series of television commercials in the 1980s while his face was issued on a postage stamp in the UK in 1985 and a counterpart featuring a caricature was used by the United States Postal Service in 1994.

The Chaplin family have also decided to keep his memory and legacy alive by converting the old family home in Switzerland into a museum. Set to include objects from his film career and personal life, the Charlie Chaplin Heritage Centre – its proposed name – is due to open its doors to the public in 2011.

■ **ABOVE:** Charlie Chaplin.
■ **RIGHT:** This 6ft statue was put up in Leicester Square three years after his death.

CITY VARIETIES
MUSIC HALL
Harry Lauder, Charlie Chaplin and
Houdini performed in this Music
Hall built in 1865 for Charles
Thornton on the site of the
White Swan coaching inn

Famous venue of the
"Good Old Days"
first broadcast,
in 1953

LEICESTER
SQUARE
WC2

LEICESTER
SQUARE WC2

Filmography

"Movies are a fad. Audiences really want to see live actors on a stage."

Charlie Chaplin made more than 80 films during his long distinguished career. I have only included those that are widely regarded as his "official" offerings and disregarded – mainly due to space – those in which he made cameo appearances as well as those that remain incomplete or unreleased.

Making a Living
Released: 2 February 1914
Character: Swindler
Plot: Wearing a top hat and a large moustache, Charlie plays Edgar English, a lady-charming swindler who runs foul of the Keystone Cops.

Kid Auto Races at Venice
Released: 7 February 1914
Character: Tramp
Plot: Chaplin's Little Tramp makes his first appearance as a spectator at a "baby-cart race" in California.

Mabel's Strange Predicament
Released: 9 February 1914
Character: Tramp
Plot: Charlie plays a drunken hotel guest who initially gets tangled in a lady's dog lead before helping Mabel who has been locked out of her room.

Between Showers
Released: 28 February 1914
Character: Masher
Plot: Chaplin and Ford Sterling play two young men who fight over the chance to help a young woman (Emma Bell Clifton) cross a muddy street.

A Film Johnnie
Released: 2 March 1914
Character: The film Johnnie
Plot: Charlie watches a movie and falls in love with a girl on screen. He goes to the studios to find her where he disrupts the shooting of a film.

Tango Tangles
Released: 9 March 1914
Character: Tipsy dancer
Plot: Charlie plays a clean-shaven drunken character who visits a dance hall where the wardrobe girl has three rival admirers fighting for her affections.

His Favourite Pastime
Released: 16 March 1914
Character: Drinker
Plot: Chaplin plays another drunken man who, this time, gets into a fight at his regular bar before following a pretty woman home, where he breaks into her house. Her husband finds Chaplin trying to seduce his wife.

Cruel, Cruel Love
Released: 26 March 1914
Character: Lord Helpus/Mr Dovey
Plot: Chaplin plays a rich lord whose romance is threatened when his girlfriend sees him being embraced by a maid in the park. He attempts to commit suicide but his butler has substituted the poison with water.

The Star Boarder
Released: 4 April 1914
Character: The star boarder
Plot: Charlie is his landlady's favourite guest which makes the other boarders jealous. A misunderstanding ends with a fight between Charlie and her husband.

Mabel at the Wheel
Released: 18 April 1914
Character: Villain
Plot: This film sees Charlie – on a motorbike – in a race with Mabel's boyfriend's car. Charlie is aided in abducting his rival, whose place is taken by Mabel herself.

Twenty Minutes of Love
Released: 20 April 1914
Character: Pickpocket
Plot: The film is set in a park among couples whose amorous antics catch his eye, leading to him embracing a tree. Confusion over a stolen pocketwatch ends up with many of the cast in the lake.

Caught in a Cabaret
Released: 27 April 1914
Character: Waiter
Plot: Charlie plays a waiter who rescues Mabel during his break, resulting in an invitation to her home. He pretends to be the Greek Ambassador but Mabel's jealous boyfriend has a plot to expose his real identity.

Caught in the Rain
Released: 4 May 1914
Character: Tipsy hotel guest
Plot: This film sees Chaplin hooking up with a lady who has become separated from her husband in the park. The

jealous husband takes out his frustration on Charlie before the action switches to the couple's hotel.

A Busy Day
Released: 7 May 1914
Character: Wife
Plot: Charlie plays a woman who is jealous of her husband and another woman. She disrupts a film set before being pushed from a pier into the harbour by her spouse.

The Fatal Mallet
Released: 1 June 1914
Character: Suitor
Plot: Three men fight for the love of a woman. Charlie plays dirty, throwing bricks and using a large hammer.

Her Friend the Bandit
Released: 4 June 1914
Character: Bandit
This 16-minute film – starring Chaplin as the Bandit, Mabel and Charles Murray

(Count De Beans) – is lost in the mists of time as there are no copies in existence.

The Knockout
Released: 11 June 1914
Character: Referee
Plot: Two tramps fake an exhibition boxing bout but Fatty Arbuckle – in the lead role – finds himself pitted against the champion. Charlie referees but the fight descends into chaos with the Keystone Kops in pursuit.

Mabel's Busy Day
Released: 13 June 1914
Character: Tipsy nuisance
Plot: Mabel plays a hotdog vendor at a car race whose wares are stolen by Chaplin. He proceeds to give them away but falls foul of the police.

Mabel's Married Life
Released: 20 June 1914
Character: Mabel's husband
Plot: Charlie hits the bottle after failing

to defend his wife's honour. Mabel, meanwhile, buys a boxing dummy for him to spar with but the drunken husband mistakes it for a real ladykiller and ends up fighting it.

Laughing Gas
Released: 9 July 1914
Character: Dentist's assistant
Plot: Mishap and mayhem at a dental surgery with Chaplin pretending to be the dentist rather than the assistant.

The Property Man
Released: 1 August 1914
Character: The property man
Plot: Charlie struggles with actors' luggage, scene changes and mistimed entries amid arguments over the star dressing room.

The Face on the Bar Room Floor
Released: 10 August 1914
Character: Artist
Plot: Loosely based on the poem of the

same name by Hugh Antoine D'Arcy, this film sees Charlie as a jilted painter who drunkenly attempts to draw a picture of the woman he loves on a bar room floor.

Recreation
Released: 13 August 1914
Character: Tramp
Plot: Charlie gets caught up in a love tryst between a seaman and his girlfriend before first ending up in a fight, and then in the water.

The Masquerader
Released: 27 August 1914
Character: Film actor/Beautiful stranger
Plot: Chaplin plays a bungling actor who is kicked off the set before returning dressed as a lady who charms the director.

His New Profession
Released: 31 August 1914
Character: Charlie
Plot: Charlie agrees to look after a couple's crippled uncle but ends up

drinking after using the invalid as a begging tool.

The Rounders
Released: 7 September 1914
Character: Reveller
Plot: Charlie and Fatty Arbuckle play two drunks – one who beats his wife, the other who is beaten by his – who live in the same hotel.

The New Janitor
Released: 14 September 1914
Character: Janitor
Plot: Charlie plays a janitor who is fired from his job after accidentally dousing his boss with water but ends up foiling a robbery and is rewarded.

Those Love Pangs
Released: 10 October 1914
Character: Masher
Plot: Charlie and his rival compete for a lady's affection with the action taking place in a park and at the movies.

Dough and Dynamite
Released: 26 October 1914
Character: Waiter
Plot: Chaplin and a fellow waiter are forced to work in the kitchen after the cooks go on strike. The striking bakers, however, hide dynamite in the dough before it is baked.

Gentlemen of Nerve
Released: 29 October 1914
Character: Impecunious track enthusiast
Plot: Charlie and a friend join Mabel and her boyfriend at a car race where, after a series of mishaps, the two stars hook up.

His Musical Career
Released: 7 November 1914
Character: Piano mover
Plot: Charlie and his partner suffer from confusion over which address they are to deliver a piano to and where they should repossess one.

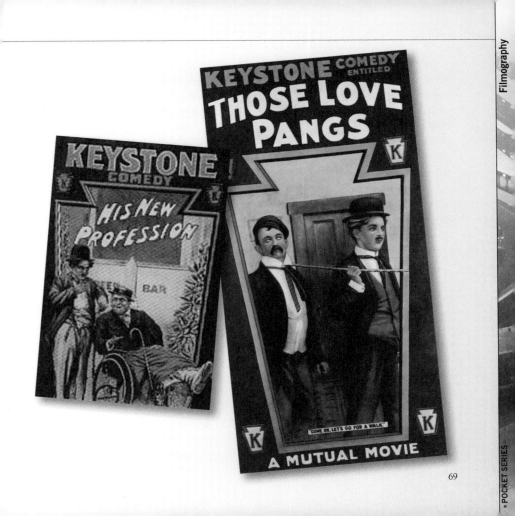

His Trysting Place
Released: 9 November 1914
Character: Husband
Plot: A mix up over coats leads to Charlie's wife thinking he has a lover and the other man's believing he has an illegitimate child.

Tillie's Punctured Romance
Released: 14 November 1914
Character: The city guy
Plot: The first feature-length comedy film from Keystone Film Company and the Christie Film Company sees Charlie persuading a wealthy farmer's daughter to elope with her father's money.

Getting Acquainted
Released: 5 December 1914
Character: Spouse
Plot: Charlie and Ambrose (Mack Swain) and their wives meet each other while walking in the park and fall for their counterparts.

His Prehistoric Past
Released: 7 December 1914
Character: Weakchin
Plot: Charlie dreams he is in the Stone Age where he falls in love with King Low-Brow's favourite wife.

His New Job
Released: 1 February 1915
Character: Film extra
Plot: Having been given the chance to help a carpenter on a movie set, Charlie ends up acting but causes chaos.

A Night Out
Released: 15 February 1915
Character: Reveller
Plot: Having caused trouble at a posh restaurant with a fellow reveller, Charlie finds himself in a series of awkward moments with the headwaiter's wife.

A Jitney Elopement
Released: 1 April 1915
Character: Suitor/Fake Count

Plot: Charlie imitates a wealthy Count at dinner whom Edna's father wishes her to marry but mayhem ensues when the real Count turns up.

The Champion
Released: 11 April 1915
Character: Challenger
Plot: After finding a lucky horseshoe while walking his dog, Charlie answers an advert for a boxing partner.

The Tramp
Released: 11 April 1915
Character: The Tramp
Plot: Charlie plays a hobo who helps a girl protect herself and her family's farm but she already has a boyfriend.

By the Sea
Released: 29 April 1915
Character: Stroller
Plot: Having fought with two husbands at a bathing resort, Charlie attempts to ingratiate himself with their wives.

Work
Released: 21 June 1915
Character: Decorator's apprentice
Plot: Charlie and his boss arrive at a couple's house but, as usual, things do not pan out smoothly with explosive results.

A Woman
Released: 12 July 1915
Character: Gentleman/Nora Nettlerash
Plot: The film is set in the park but soon Charlie is invited for dinner and ends up rushing upstairs to shave his moustache off and dress like a woman.

The Bank
Released: 9 August 1915
Character: Janitor
Plot: An inept janitor, Charlie is jilted in love but dreams of foiling a bank robbery.

Shanghaied
Released: 4 October 1915
Character: Charlie
Plot: Charlie, in love with a shipowner's

daughter, promises to help the captain shanghai a crew for a final voyage.

In the Park
Released: 18 November 1915
Character: Charlie
Plot: A tramp causes trouble by stealing a woman's handbag with her boyfriend ending up in the lake.

A Night in the Show
Released: 20 November 1915
Character: Mr Pest/Mr Rowdy
Plot: Chaplin plays two disruptive theatregoers who fight the conductor and attack the patrons and entertainers.

A Burlesque on Carmen
Released: 18 December 1915
Character: Darn Hosiery
Plot: A parody of Bizet's Carmen, Chaplin plays a Spanish officer seduced by a gypsy girl.

The Floorwalker
Released: 15 May 1916
Character: Tramp
Plot: Mayhem in a department store leads to Charlie confronting a mirror image in a store inspector who has just robbed the safe. This film is notable for the first to use a "running staircase" to enhance the slapstick comedy.

Police
Released: 27 May 1916
Character: Ex-convict
Plot: Charlie is released from prison only to find himself the victim of a swindle at the hands of a fake parson before being persuaded to commit burglary.

The Fireman
Released: 12 June 1916
Character: Fireman
Plot: After a house owner persuades the fire chief to ignore his burning home because he wants to claim the insurance, Charlie saves the day… and the man's daughter.

The Vagabond
Released: 10 July 1916
Character: Street musician
Plot: A down on his luck violinist, Chaplin saves a girl from a band of gypsies but becomes embroiled in a love triangle.

One AM
Released: 7 August 1916
Character: Drunk
Plot: In the first film in which he starred alone, Chaplin plays the role of a drunk homeowner who wants to go to bed, but the inanimate objects around him prevent him.

The Count
Released: 4 September 1916
Character: Tailor's apprentice
Plot: After Chaplin burns the Count's trousers, the tailor discovers the Count won't be attending a party and goes himself instead. Charlie ends up at the same address as the Count.

The Pawnshop
Released: 2 October 1916
Character: Pawnbroker's assistant
Plot: Charlie proves inept as a pawnbroker's shop assistant but ends up capturing a burglar.

Behind the Screen
Released: 13 November 1916
Character: Property man's assistant
Plot: Chaplin is a scene shifter at a film studio where the other shifters go on strike with three movies in production. Charlie eventually falls for a girl dressed as a man.

The Rink
Released: 4 December 1916
Character: Waiter/posing as Sir Cecil Seltzer
Plot: Chaplin goes roller skating during his lunch break from the restaurant and showcases his excellent skills before being invited to a party at Edna's.

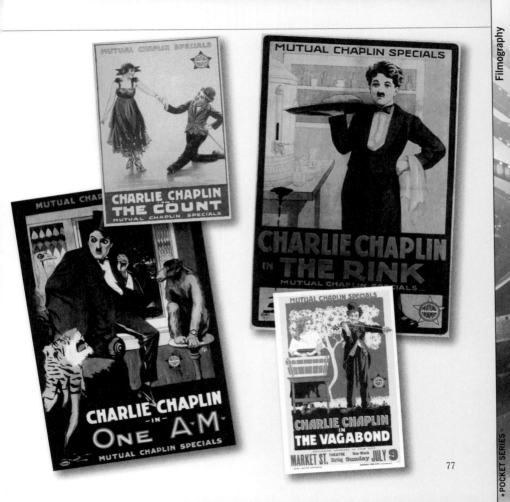

77

Easy Street
Released: 22 January 1917
Character: Vagabond recruited to police force
Plot: From sleeping outside a mission, Chaplin is transformed into a policeman taking on a bully and rescuing a damsel in distress.

The Cure
Released: 16 April 1917
Character: Alcoholic gentleman at spa
Plot: Laughter and mayhem when a drunk – with a suitcase full of alcohol – checks into a health spa to dry out.

The Immigrant
Released: 17 June 1917
Character: Immigrant
Plot: The film charts an immigrant's voyage to America and his arrival in the States, with trials and tribulations due to a lack of money.

The Adventurer
Released: 22 October 1917
Character: Escaped convict
Plot: Chaplin stars as an escaped convict who saves a young lady from drowning. He is taken in but needs to evade the attentions of the pursuing prison guards.

A Dog's Life
Released: 14 April 1918
Character: Tramp
Plot: Chaplin, a tramp, rescues a dog from other strays and together they strive to make their – and dancehall singer Edna's – lives better. This film saw Chaplin's brother Sydney play a small role, the first time the two had appeared on screen together.

Triple Trouble
Released: 11 August 1918
Character: Janitor
Plot: Chaplin plays a janitor who joins an inventor's household who helps

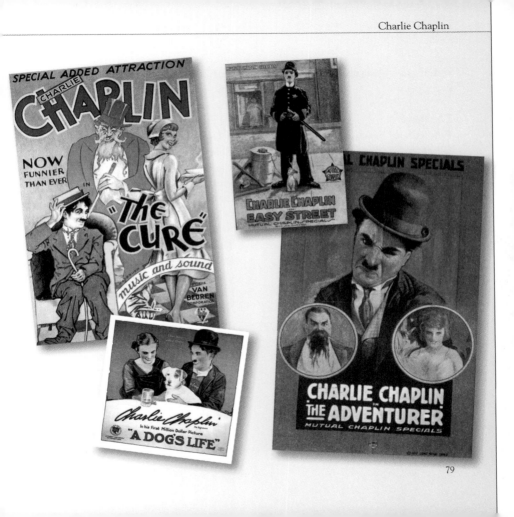

thwart plans to steal his boss's explosive experiments.

The Bond
Released: 29 September 1918
Character: Himself
Plot: A series of short sketches that highlight bonds such as friendship, love and marriage as well as Liberty Bonds which will knock out the Kaiser.

Shoulder Arms
Released: 20 October 1918
Character: Recruit
Plot: Chaplin's shortest feature film at 46 minutes, this is set in France during the First World War and includes a piece of Limburger cheese that necessitates a gas mask as well as the hero disguising himself as a tree in enemy lines.

Sunnyside
Released: 15 May 1919
Character: Farm handyman
Plot: Charlie plays a handyman in love with his neighbour's daughter who encounters a rival in the form of a city slicker.

A Day's Pleasure
Released: 15 December 1919
Character: Father
Plot: Chaplin takes his family for a day's outing, suffering trouble with their car before enjoying an excursion on a boat.

The Kid
Released: 6 February 1921
Character: Tramp
Plot: Chaplin discovers an abandoned baby boy who grows up to help the tramp's criminal activities before eventually being reunited with his mother.

The Idle Class
Released: 25 September 1921
Character: Tramp/Husband
Plot: Chaplin plays a tramp who gatecrashes a posh golf resort where he is mistaken for a rich woman's husband.

Pay Day
Released: 2 April 1922
Character: Labourer
Plot: Chaplin's final two-reel short film sees him play an expert bricklayer trying to outwit his wife to go to the saloon.

The Pilgrim
Released: 26 February 1923
Character: Escaped convict
Plot: Chaplin steals a minister's clothing and ends up being mistaken for the parson before trying to reform a fellow criminal.

A Woman of Paris
Released: 26 September 1923
Character: Porter
Plot: Written, produced and directed by Chaplin, this film about a woman who believes she has been jilted by her artist fiancé only starred its creator in a small role.

The Gold Rush
Released: 26 June 1925
Character: Lone prospector

Plot: Chaplin heads for Alaska in search of gold but encounters some troublesome characters and falls in love.

The Circus
Released: 6 January 1928
Character: Tramp
Plot: Having been mistaken for a pickpocket, Chaplin's character enters a circus tent to evade the police but the ringmaster puts his comic skills to work.

City Lights
Released: 6 February 1931
Character: Tramp
Plot: A blind flowergirl mistakes Chaplin for a wealthy Duke but it is the tramp who raises enough money to restore her sight.

Modern Times
Released: 5 February 1936
Character: Worker
Plot: Chaplin's final "silent" film sees him struggling to cope with new technology in the form of a production line.

The Great Dictator
Released: 15 October 1940
Character: Adenoid Hynkel/Barber
Plot: Nominated for Academy Awards for Best Actor and Best Writing (Original Screenplay), Chaplin plays a barber who is mistaken for a dictator in this satire of Adolf Hitler.

Monsieur Verdoux
Released: 11 April 1947
Character: Monsieur Henri Verdoux
Plot: Again nominated for an Academy Award for Best Writing (Original Screenplay), Chaplin plays an unemployed banker who marries wealthy widows before murdering them.

Limelight
Released: 16 October 1952
Character: Calvero
Plot: Set in London in 1914, Charlie plays a washed-up clown who saves a young dancer from committing suicide.

They both attempt to revive their careers with differing results.

A King in New York
Released: 12 September 1957
Character: King Shahdov
Plot: This film echoes Chaplin's experiences in being exiled from America with King Shahdov relocating due to a revolution and finding himself accused of being a suspected Communist.

A Countess from Hong Kong
Released: 5 January 1967
Character: An old steward
Plot: An ambassador-designate meets a Russian countess in Hong Kong who is fleeing being forced into prostitution. This was Chaplin's final outing as director and his cameo appearance marks his farewell to the silver screen. It did, however, feature his second son Sydney Earle Chaplin.

■ **ABOVE:** Just after Sir Charlie Chaplin was knighted, with his family.

Awards and Recognition

"Actors search for rejection. If they don't get it they reject themselves."

While the majority of people involved in motion pictures crave awards and the subsequent recognition they bring, Charlie Chaplin was not stereotypical of the industry. Indeed, he held the Academy Awards (Oscars) in disdain and joked about using his golden statue as a doorstop. It did not, however, prevent the awards from piling up.

The diminutive Londoner was knighted by Queen Elizabeth II at the age of 85, just two years before his death. Making him Sir Charlie Chaplin – Knight Commander of the British Empire (KBE) – had first been proposed more

■ **TOP:** Kodak Theatre in LA.
■ **ABOVE:** Charlie Chaplin holding his honorary Oscar.

than 40 years earlier but it was felt by the powers that be at the time that his moral reputation (in marrying two 16 year olds) and his alleged political views would not reflect well on Great Britain and its relationship with the United States.

Academy Awards

Film	Year	Result	Award	Category/Recipient(s)
The Circus (1928)	1929		Honorary Award	*
The Great Dictator (1940)	1941	Nominated	Oscar	Best Actor in a Leading Role
The Great Dictator (1940)	1941	Nominated	Oscar	Best Writing, Original Screenplay
Monsieur Verdoux (1947)	1948	Nominated	Oscar	Best Writing, Original Screenplay
N/A	1972		Honorary Award	**
Limelight (1952)	1973	Won	Oscar	Best Music, Original Dramatic Score ***

BAFTA Awards

Film	Year	Result	Award	Category/Recipient(s)
N/A	1977		Academy Fellowship	

■ **ABOVE:** Charlie Chaplin meeting Queen Elizabeth after receiving the Acadamy Fellowship from BAFTA.

Blue Ribbon Awards

Film	Year	Result	Award	Category/Recipient(s)
Monsieur Verdoux (1947)	1953	Won	Blue Ribbon	Best Foreign Language Film

Bodil Awards

Film	Year	Result	Award	Category/Recipient(s)
Monsieur Verdoux (1947)	1949	Won	Bodil	Best American Film
N/A	1959		Honorary Award	

Directors Guild of America, USA

Film	Year	Result	Award	Category/Recipient(s)
N/A	1974		DGA Honorary Life Member Award	

Film Society of Lincoln Centre

Film	Year	Result	Award	Category/Recipient(s)
N/A	1972		Gala Tribute	

Italian National Syndicate of Film Journalists

Film	Year	Result	Award	Category/Recipient(s)
Limelight (1952)	1953	Won	Silver Ribbon	Best Foreign Film

Jussi Awards

Film	Year	Result	Award	Category/Recipient(s)
Modern Times (1936)	1974	Won	Jussi	Best Foreign Filmmaker

Kinema Junpo Awards

Film	Year	Result	Award	Category/Recipient(s)
A Woman of Paris (1923)	1925	Won	Kinema Junpo	Best Artistic Film
The Gold Rush (1925)	1927	Won	Kinema Junpo	Best Foreign Language Film

Awards and Recognition

Film	Year	Result	Award	Category/Recipient(s)
Monsieur Verdoux (1947)	1953	Won	Kinema Junpo	Best Foreign Language Film
The Great Dictator (1940)	1961	Won	Kinema Junpo	Best Foreign Language Film

New York Film Critics Circle Awards

Film	Year	Result	Award	Category/Recipient(s)
The Great Dictator (1940)	1940	Won	NYFCC	Best Actor

Venice Film Festival

Film	Year	Result	Award	Category/Recipient(s)
N/A	1972	Won	Career Golden Lion	

Walk of Fame

Film	Year	Result	Award	Category/Recipient(s)
N/A	1970		Star on the Walk of Fame	Motion Picture ****

*For versatility and genius in acting, writing, directing and producing The Circus. The film was originally nominated in the Best Actor category, but the Academy decided to remove Chaplin's name from the competitive classes.

**For the incalculable effect Chaplin had in making motion pictures the art form of the century.

***The film was not released in Los Angeles until 1972.

****At 6751 Hollywood Boulevard.

90

■ **ABOVE:** Charlie Chaplin after receiving an Honorary Doctor of Letters degree.

POCKET SERIES

Charlie Chaplin in Popular Culture

> **"A tramp, a gentleman, a poet, a dreamer, a lonely fellow, always hopeful of romance and adventure."**

It is a testament to the genius of Charlie Chaplin that his is still an instantly recognisable face and a household name in the 21st Century as the centenary of his cinematic debut approaches. While his films may not be repeated on television as often as they have been in the past, it is possible to enjoy his magic through the numerous DVDs available.

Such is the interest in the man himself, that a biopic was released in 1992. Directed by Richard Attenborough and starring Robert Downey Jr in the title role, *Chaplin* found great acclaim with the

■ **RIGHT:** Robert Downey Jr.

majority of critics and moviegoers alike and was nominated for three Academy Awards – Best Actor in a Leading Role, Best Art Direction-Set Decoration and Best Music, Original Score – but emerged empty-handed. Downey did, however, pick up the Best Actor trophy at the BAFTA (British Academy of Film and Television Arts) Awards while the film was nominated for a plethora of awards throughout the film industry.

Chaplin has also been the subject of many a thesis over the decades, although a more in-depth analysis occurred when Charles J Maland examined Chaplin's relationship with his adopted land in *Chaplin and American Culture* (published by Princeton University Press in 1991). It debates how and why Chaplin fell from grace (and was rehabilitated), both as a film artist and as a public figure.

But it's not just the literary community that has a reverence for Charlie Chaplin; his musical scores have been lauded as well, particularly one

■ **ABOVE:** Nat King Cole.

song from *Modern Times*. The score was composed by Chaplin – a violinist with some musical knowledge – and arranged with the assistance of Alfred Newman. The romance theme was later given lyrics and went on to become the pop standard "Smile", first recorded by Nat King Cole and later covered by such artists as Barbra Streisand, Diana Ross, Michael Bublé, Petula Clark, Liberace and Judy Garland. It was also the favourite of the King of Pop, Michael Jackson, who recorded a version for his "HIStory" double album in 1995. Long-time friend Brooke Shields revealed the song's special place in Jackson's heart at his 2009 memorial service while Michael's brother Jermaine sang a heart-tugging rendition.

It now seems, though, that a new generation of children are soon to be introduced to a 21st Century Charlie Chaplin with the announcement in January 2010 that animation companies in India and France will be teaming up to create a computer-generated version

■ **ABOVE:** Tommy Steele in the padding required to do the stunts for his role as a young Charlie Chaplin.

of The Tramp. With an estimated budget of £7 million, they are hoping to produce more than 100 six-minute episodes (available from early 2011) that aim to keep in tradition with Chaplin's persona but which are set in modern situations.

Let's hope that those charged with honouring Charlie Chaplin's memory pay heed to his words: "I suppose that's one of the ironies of life, doing the wrong thing at the right moment… In the end, everything is a gag."

■ **ABOVE:** Twiggy with a wax work of Chaplin and Joe Geary, a child actor who played Chaplin on television.